SOUND OF SILENCE

SWATI MISALA

BookLeaf Publishing

India | USA | UK

Made with ❤ on the BookLeaf Publishing Platform
www.bookleafpub.in
www.bookleafpub.com

Dedication

For the dreamers, the wanderers, and the ones who feel everything too deeply.

For those who find poetry in the quiet moments, in the chaos, in the love and the loss.

And for you—whoever you are, wherever you are—may these words find you when you need them most.

With love,
swati

Preface

Poetry has always been a sanctuary—This collection is a reflection of moments captured in verse, a journey through love and loss, hope and despair, quiet contemplation and loud awakening.

Each poem within these pages was born from the rawness of life itself. Some were written in solitude, where words whispered their way onto the page, while others emerged from encounters with the world, shaped by the voices of people and places that left their mark on me. In these lines, you may find fragments of your own story—echoes of emotions you've felt, dreams you've chased, or questions you've pondered.

This book is not meant to dictate meaning but to invite exploration. Read it in sequence, or open it at random and let the words find you. Allow yourself to linger in the spaces between the lines, where poetry breathes its quiet truths.

Above all, I hope these poems offer you what they have given me—a sense of connection, a moment of stillness, and perhaps even the courage to embrace the beauty and complexity of being human.

With gratitude,
Swati

Acknowledgements

This collection would not have been possible without the love, support, and inspiration of so many people.

To my Parents —thank you for believing in me.Your unwavering support means everything.

To my Husband for encouraging my words when I doubted them, and for always reminding me why I write.

Special thanks to Ruchi madam for sharing this 21 Days challenge with me.

To the poets and artists who have inspired me—your words have shaped my own, and I am grateful for the paths you have paved.

To my readers—thank you for taking the time to sit with these poems, to feel them, to find meaning in them. Poetry is a conversation, and I am honored to share this space with you.

And finally, to the moments—both light and dark—that have filled these pages, thank you for teaching me, for shaping me, and for giving me something to write about.

With gratitude,
Swati

1. ALONE

When you find yourself standing alone..,

On a lost road or a path unshown..
With a heart that's scared and fear unknown !

Just look in the mirror and hold yourself...,
look in the mirror and let go of that frown..

Remember what brought you here,
Remember how much you've grown!

2. LEFT ALONE WITH MY THOUGHTS

As soon as I was left alone with my thoughts..

The past was reviewed,
Future was questioned.
What's to be left...
What should be pursued!!!
Had it made any sense ?
Does it really make any difference??
This thought is going too deep
Should I leave it now? or should I proceed!
I can never forget how that made me feel ..
Ahh..let it go it's no big deal.
As soon I was left alone with my thoughts
My head was blown
My heart was torn.

~By an overthinking anxious person.

3. EMPEROR OF HER OWN DREAMS

They told her to dream

To dream of a king and a Castle
To dream to be the Queen...

Little do they know...She don't need no king or a Castle...
She don't dream to be the Queen...
She desires to build her own mansion and a throne that
gleams...
She don't need no king or a castle...

FOR SHE IS THE EMPEROR OF HER DREAMS

4. SOUND OF SILENCE

If only the silence could speak It would have told a story,
Maybe few tales to preach....
Withholding thousand words and
No one to reach...
Is it hiding a truth ,or a promise to keep?
Or is it afraid to spill the mystical love of winter and
breeze...
If only the silence could speak It would have told a story,
Maybe few tales to preach.

5. LOST IN THE CROWD

Do you feel lost in the crowd..?
Want to be heard but the noises too loud.

Waving you from a distance is a fear of tomorrow..
How much sanity can you incur ?
How much you need to borrow !!

Do you too feel lost in the crowd ..

Want to be heard but the noises too loud.

6. BROKEN

She had been broken quite a few times now..

Broken by the winds that did not took her anguish away...,

Broken by the stars that didn't shined her way.

Broken by the eyes that did not wait for her,

Broken by the smiles that couldn't mask her tears...

Broken by the lies that she believed over all these years ...

Broken by the time that perished so fast...

Broken by the pieces she was collecting all her way from past.

7. OLDEN TIMES

From the dewy scents of morning rain,..

Bestowed upon the memories down that childhood lane...

Took me to the olden times ...

Where I could be heedless yet fierce !!!

Where I could be myself again.

8. WHAT WILL PEOPLE SAY

WHAT WILL PEOPLE SAY

They showed her Colors that define her, but she chose what
she loved ,she chose grey...

She built her own castle that gleams of pride night and day...

For she no longer fear to walk away ,

She no longer feared what they think..
She no longer feared what will people say.

9. THOUSAND STORIES

If only I were there,
I would've held your hand
I would've let you stare...

For this Farness has kept us longing for love,
Love that we had...
Was it love?
Or was it just sweet innocent lies wrapped in love ,I
don't care.

I will tell you thousand stories,
If we ever meet again I swear!

If we ever meet again,
If I see you there,
I will hold your hand
I will let you stare.

10. CLOSE ~ APART

They were close... they were apart,
Drenched in love were their hearts

Holding on to what's left so far

Like winds trying to touch the sea...

Like roots trying to hold the tree...

Latching on to what's left,

Few memories that were precious
Thousand moments to be kept.

They were close...they were apart
Drenched in love were their hearts.

11. ROOTS OF LOVE

Who you are, what you are to me?
Will you make me fly,
Will you set me free?
The sense of that touch,
the warmth of that first kiss...
How will I forget that smile,
Oh heavenly bliss!!
I will remember the music in your eyes,
The times you've told me how magical I was...
And when you held my hand amidst the Misty winter
night,
I can never forget that esthetic sight!
So hold me tight,
And let it be....
For the roots of love will always cherish its tree.
For the roots of love will always cherish its tree.

12. THESE LAST FEW MEMORIES I HAVE OF YOU.

Walking alone on the seashore, thinking of you....

This Heart still yearns for that last glance of you....

Walking alone on the sand, looking at the stars....
Not wanting this night to end...
Don't want this night to end..

For tomorrow might be hard...
Tomorrow will be blue...
Tomorrow may steal away from me

THESE LAST FEW MEMORIES I HAVE OF YOU.

13. LET GO

Let go oh darling Let go of pain,
Let go of fear,
Let go of things, don't let your soul tear ...
Let go of pain,
Let your heart melt, let the tears of fright pour into the
thoughts of rain...
Let go of pain,
Let the shadows of worry scatter .....they can't be
contained
Let go oh darling
Let go of pain,
Don't hold it tight ...don't let it cause strain...
Let go oh darling
Let go of pain...

14. CRISP BREEZE OF DECEMBER

You will meet a lot of people on your way,
Many will give you memories
Some will give you reasons to stay!

Many will laugh with you...
Some will cry for you
Few will take your sorrows away.
Many will teach you lessons
Some will become your precious possessions.

But, everyone you meet will give you something to
remember....
Many will become the heat wave of summer...

Some will be like calm crisp breeze of December!

15. BLITHE

Once there was a bird herce ...blithe .,..alone

No winds could take away her home.!

Light in her eyes could tell a story,

With a smile that's fearless...and a soul that never felt
sorry .!!

Then came a storm along with the thunder that was
glaring...,

Torn up her home ...as she started caring.

16. A LOVE LIKE THAT

Look for love that is more than just mystery & more
than pleasure,

Look for love that you'll want to keep you'll want to
treasure ....

Seek for love that don't scatter like sand in storm of vain,

A Love that"ll hold you together and sink to the bottom
like Rain....

Yearn for love that don't just water your vine,

But will grow with it, till the end of time.

17. TILL YOU FALL

As soon as this anger dissolve.,.

And you will be left with a heart that no longer stand tall....

With the distance too appalling

& agony that will make you recall...

Every second „.every minute

Till you feel shredded...

Till you falL.

18. DESIRE

There are bits of her that refuse to heal..
&
in the moments of distress they are ready to reveal.

She carry in her heart depths of emotions,
Some came with a baggage of wistful past and few with
illusory notion's!

Got burnt every time she approached the fire...

When to feel the warmth was her only desire!!!

19. CORE

For all those empty sleepless nights,

And for the days you picked yourself up but can no
longer fight

When you find yourself in an endless tunnel
And you lost all hope and there is too much struggle !

When they told you to not be hard on yourself,
And it shall too pass ... it's just a process.

Look at yourself... look in the mirror,
What scares you most, what do you fear...

What makes it hard, what made it tough
Was it about the time someone made you feel that you
are not enough?

20. GOODBYE

And tomorrow if we say goodbye...
Remember the promises we made ,
Remember the laughter we shared !

Remember how you made me laugh,
How I prayed for you on god's behalf.

How shattered I was before I met you,
How you fixed this heart even before I let you!

How everything around you just felt alright....
You were the warmth of sunny days to my cold winter
nights.

And tomorrow if we say goodbye.

Remember the promises we made
Remember the laughter we shared.

21. UNSCARRED

When the words start to sound bitter,

And I am lost in the world that no longer glitter....

Find me a better place .....unscarred...unscathed,

A place where I could reach

Where I could find someone to hold ...,

the one I could preach!

22. TO THE ONE WHO CAUSED THE PAIN

I promise those wounds feel fresh, every time they hit
the rain..

It triggers on a brisk winter night or an afternoon so
mundane ,..

There is only much a soul can contain ,..

To the one who caused the pain ...

I promise these wounds feel fresh again, every time they
hit the rain.

23. FEARLESS

She was like wind..fearless.. erratic „flowing everywhere

He was like a mountain.. stable...sane, rooted to the ground

Now what will you call a love like that!

24. FREE

And I put it all behind me...
As I walked passed the fiery lanes
of destiny.,.
flaunting the scars of past,
Carrying the burden of what it could be..
Piece by piece
Drop by drop
I put it all behind me...
I was finally free!

25. PRESERVE THE BLUES

Into the deep blue ocean of thoughts, lies
Rare reds of agony and few hints of troubling hues,
All trying to collide, Striving to fuse ...
Now will they cause distress?
Or will they diffuse.
Will the ocean surrender himself?
Or will he fight to preserve the blues.

26. SILENT BENCH

The rocks I put under one silent bench,..
Those rocks I put every time under that silent bench..,
Hiding few anxious puddles covering one painful
trench!!
Are ready to cluster...
and once hit by the storm
They soon will fluster!!!
The rocks I put under my silent bench.

27. DAD

You taught me how to be kind,
And when I fell you held me up, you stood behind

You always told me how much you are proud ,
And never let me question myself you never let me
doubt.

And today Is when we thank you for all the sacrifices
you made night and day...

And not just today your love should be
celebrated everyday.

www.ingramcontent.com/pod-product-compliance
Lightning Source LLC
LaVergne TN
LVHW010952200726

843509LV00013B/2386